Look After Yourself

Healthy Teeth

Angela Royston

Heinemann Library
Chicago, Illinois

Designed by Dave Oakley
Photo research by Helen Reilly
Originated by Dot Gradations Ltd
Printed and bound in China by South China Printing Company

07 06 05 04 03
10 9 8 7 6 5 4 3 2 1

Library of Congress Cataloging-in-Publication Data
Royston, Angela.
  Healthy teeth / Angela Royston.
       v. cm. -- (Look after yourself)
Includes bibliographical references and index.
Contents: Your body -- Different kinds of teeth -- Inside a tooth --
Sweet and sticky food -- Sugary drinks -- Brushing your teeth --
How to brush your teeth -- Check your toothbrush! -- Feed your teeth!
 -- Your baby teeth -- See your dentist regularly -- Take care of your
permanent teeth.
  ISBN 1-4034-4443-9 (lib. bdg.) -- ISBN 1-4034-4452-8 (pbk.)
  1. Teeth--Care and hygiene--Juvenile literature.
[1. Teeth--Care and hygiene.] I. Title.
  RK63.R695 2003
  617.6'01--dc21

                                      2003001001

Acknowledgments
The author and publisher are grateful to the following for permission to reproduce copyright material:
Cover photograph by Pauline Cutler/Bubbles.
p. 4 Gareth Boden; pp. 5, 6, 12, 13, 14, 15, 17, 18, 19, 20, 21, 25 Trevor Clifford; p. 7 Pascal Goethghelack/Science Photo Library; p. 8 BSIP Laurent/Science Photo Library; pp. 10, 16–17, 22, 26, 27 Powerstock; p. 11 BSIP VEM/Science Photo Library; p. 23 Martin Barraud/Getty Images; p. 24 Hattie Young/Science Photo Library.

Special thanks to David Wright for his help in the preparation of this book.

Some words are shown in bold, **like this.** You can find out what they mean by looking in the glossary.

Contents

Your Body

Your body is made up of many parts that work together. Each part has a special job to do. Your teeth chew up the food you need to keep healthy and stay alive.

Your teeth break up food into small pieces that are easy to **swallow.** This book is about teeth and how to keep them healthy.

Different Kinds of Teeth

Your front teeth are sharp and flat like knives. They are called **incisors.** You use them to take a bite.

Your **canines** are long and sharp. They grip food. The back teeth, called **molars,** are wider with a bumpy top. They grind up food.

canine

incisor

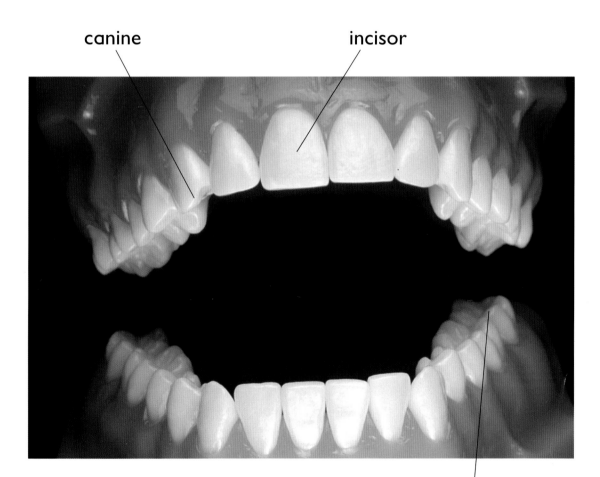

molar

Inside a Tooth

Your teeth grow out of your **jawbone.** They have roots surrounded by your **gums.** You need to take care of your gums as well as your teeth.

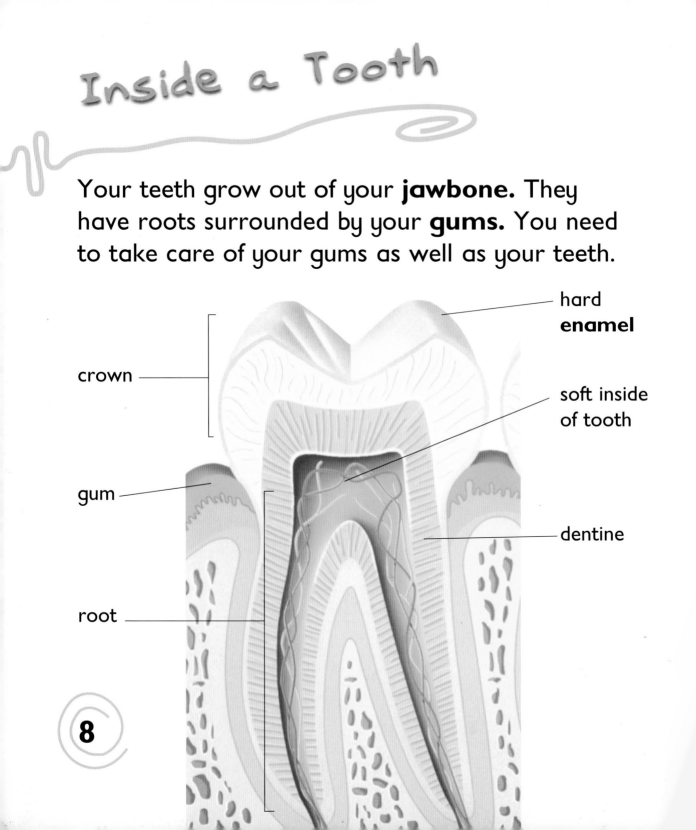

hard
enamel

crown

soft inside
of tooth

gum

dentine

root

A layer of hard enamel covers each tooth. If this enamel wears away, you may get a hole in your tooth called a **cavity.** If the cavity is deep, your tooth aches a lot.

9

Sweet and Sticky Food

Sugar hurts your teeth. When you eat something sweet or sticky, some of the sugar sticks to your teeth. **Germs** in your mouth feed on the sugar.

The germs make **acid** that can make a hole in the **enamel.** A dentist can fix the hole by putting a **filling** in it.

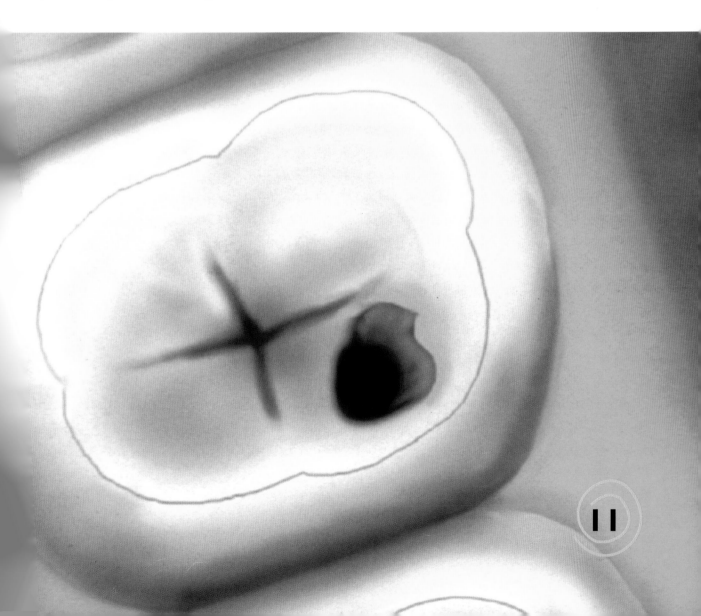

Sugary Drinks

Cola and other soft drinks contain a lot of sugar. So does fruit juice. The sugar washes around your mouth and sticks to your teeth.

If you do have a sweet drink, have a glass of water afterwards. The water will help wash some of the sugar off of your teeth and **gums.**

Brushing Your Teeth

You should brush your teeth at least twice a day. Brushing your teeth sweeps away any bits of food or **germs** that stay on your teeth after you eat.

14

You should brush your teeth before you go to bed. Try to brush them after each meal. Then, try not to eat anything after you have brushed your teeth.

How to Brush Your Teeth

When you brush your
teeth, you should brush
down from the **gum**
to the tip of each
tooth. Brush the back
and the front of
each tooth.

Brushing helps get rid of food
and **germs** between your teeth
and under your gums.
Finally, brush the
tops of your
back teeth.
Brush your teeth
for at least
two minutes.

17

Check Your Toothbrush!

Are the **bristles** of your toothbrush **firm** and straight? Your toothbrush cannot do a good job if the bristles are bent like the ones in this picture.

You should only use a toothbrush for a few months. Then you should get a new one. You will also need a new one if you have been taking **medicine** for an **infection**.

Feed Your Teeth!

Carrots, apples, and other raw fruits and vegetables are good for your teeth. They help your teeth stay sharp and strong.

20

These foods are also good for your teeth. They contain a **mineral** called **calcium.** Calcium makes your teeth grow strong.

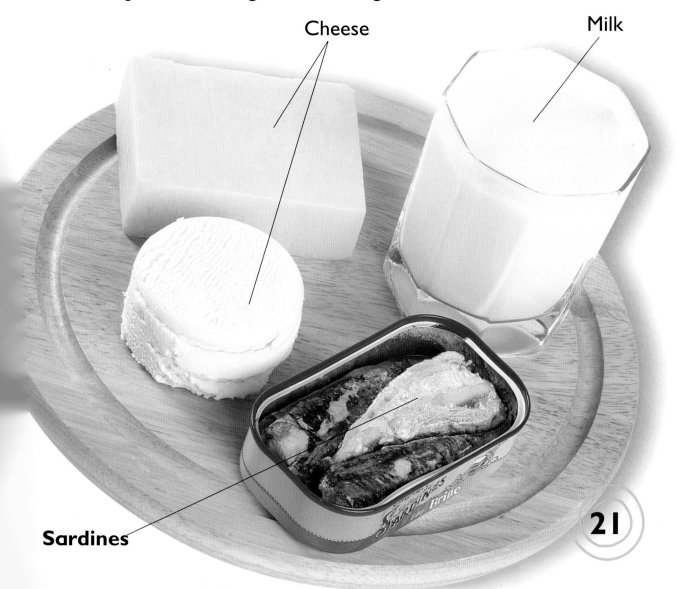

Cheese

Milk

Sardines

Your Baby Teeth

Your first set of teeth are called baby teeth. When you are about five or six years old, your baby teeth begin to fall out. Bigger teeth grow in their place.

Some baby teeth fall out easily. Some need to be pulled out by an adult. When a baby tooth falls out, it makes room for a **permanent** tooth.

You should see a dentist every six months. The dentist will make sure that your teeth are healthy. If one of your teeth has a **cavity,** the dentist will put in a **filling.**

26

The dentist will also make sure that your **permanent** teeth are growing well. The dentist may put **fluoride** on your teeth to make the **enamel** stronger.

I've been to the Dentist!

Take Care of Your Permanent Teeth

Permanent means "meant to last." Your permanent teeth should last your whole life. If you lose one of your permanent teeth, you cannot grow another one.

If a permanent tooth gets hurt or broken, a dentist can make you a false tooth. Many older people have false teeth.

It's a Fact!

Baby teeth and **permanent** teeth begin to form in your **gums** before you are born. Permanent teeth begin to come in as your baby teeth fall out.

It is important to eat foods that contain **calcium,** to make your teeth strong. **Sardines, okra,** broccoli, white bread, and milk all contain calcium.

There are millions of **germs** in your mouth. Germs can hurt your teeth and your gums. Your gums should be a soft pink color. If they are red or puffy, you should see your dentist.

It is important to clean between your teeth. The best way to clean between teeth that are close together is to use **dental floss.** This is a kind of thread that you pull backward and forward between your teeth. Your dentist can show you how to use it.

Most toothpastes contain **fluoride.** Toothpaste also contains powdered chalk and a kind of soap. The chalk helps to scrub your teeth and the soap makes them clean.

Fluoride makes your teeth really strong if you swallow it while your teeth are forming. Some tap water has fluoride added to it. If the water you drink does not contain fluoride, you can take fluoride drops every day.

Glossary

acid chemical that can make holes in solids, such as metals or teeth

bristle short, stiff spike on a brush

calcium mineral that makes your teeth and bones strong and hard

canine sharp, pointed tooth that you use to hold onto food

cavity hole in a tooth caused by acid in the mouth

dental floss type of thread used to clean food out from between teeth

enamel hard, shiny covering on each tooth

filling metal or other substance a dentist uses to fix a cavity in a tooth

firm almost hard

fluoride mineral that makes your teeth stronger and more able to fight off acid in your mouth

germ tiny living thing that attacks different parts of the body

gum flesh that covers your jawbone and the roots of your teeth

incisor   tooth at the front of your mouth that you use to cut food

infection   sickness, such as a sore throat, caused by germs

jawbone   hinged bone that your teeth grow out of

medicine   substance used to treat an illness

mineral   chemical that is contained in some foods and that your body needs to stay healthy

molar   wide tooth at the back of your mouth that you use to grind up food

okra   kind of vegetable that consists of a sticky green pod and seeds

permanent   lasting

sardine   small sea fish

swallow   push food from your mouth down your throat

More Books to Read

Bagley, Katie. *Brush Well: A Look at Dental Care.* Mankato, Minn.: Bridgestone Books, 2001.

Fowler, Allan. *A Look at Teeth.* Danbury, Conn.: Children's Press, 2000.

Vogel, Elizabeth. *Brushing My Teeth.* New York: PowerKids Press, 2001.

31

Index